D1123334

Serving Your Country

The Golden Knights:

The U.S. Army Parachute Team

by Ellen Hopkins

CAPSTONE
HIGH-INTEREST
BOOKS

an imprint of Capstone Press
Mankato, Minnesota

Capstone High-Interest Books are published by Capstone Press
151 Good Counsel Drive, P.O. Box 669, Mankato, Minnesota 56002
http://www.capstone-press.com

Library of Congress Cataloging-in-Publication Data
Hopkins, Ellen.
    The Golden Knights: the U.S. Army parachute team/by Ellen Hopkins.
    p. cm.—(Serving your country)
    Includes bibliographical references (p. 45) and index.
    ISBN 0-7368-0775-6
    1. United States. Army. Parachute Team—Juvenile literature. 2. Parachuting—
United States—Juvenile literature. 3. Skydiving—United States—Juvenile literature.
[1. United States. Army. Parachute Team. 2. Parachuting. 3. Skydiving.] I. Title.
II. Series.
UD483 .H67 2001
797.5'6'0973—dc21
                                                                    00-009823

Summary: Describes the U.S. Army Golden Knights, their history, mission, maneuvers, and team members.

Editorial Credits
Blake Hoena, editor; Lois Wallentine, product planning editor; Timothy Halldin,
    cover designer; Linda Clavel, illustrator and production designer; Katy Kudela,
    photo researcher

Photo Credits
Defense Visual Information Center, 10, 13, 17, 18
Ed Ponikwia, 30, 35
Matt Swinden, 23, 26, 36
The Image Finders/Michael Evans, 4
Unicorn Stock Photos/Terry Barner, cover; Dennis Thompson, 6; Michael Massey, 21
USAPT, Media Relations Office, 24, 28, 32, 40, 43
Visuals Unlimited/L. S. Stepanowicz, 15

Photo on page 38 provided courtesy of Dana and Jennifer Bowman,
www.danabowman.com.

1 2 3 4 5 6 06 05 04 03 02 01

**Capstone Press would like to thank the U.S. Army Golden Knights for their help
and support.**

Table of Contents

Chapter 1
The Golden Knights

The U.S. Army Parachute Team (USAPT) begins its performances 12,500 feet (3,810 meters) above the ground. One team member jumps out of a C-31A Troopship airplane as it passes over the air show's audience. Unlike many military demonstration teams, USAPT members do not perform by flying airplanes. Instead, they jump out of them using parachutes. These pieces of strong, lightweight fabric allow people to jump from airplanes and safely land on the ground. USAPT members are called Golden Knights.

More Golden Knights prepare to jump as the first parachutist lands. The first parachutist is

The Golden Knights parachute from airplanes.

The Golden Knights attach smoke canisters to their feet for air shows.

also known as the narrator. This team member tells the audience about the Golden Knights and the maneuvers that they will perform.

The remaining Golden Knights free fall toward the ground. They may reach speeds of up to 150 miles (240 kilometers) per hour as they fall.

The Golden Knights have smoke canisters attached to their feet. These containers release red smoke. The smoke allows audiences to see the Golden Knights as they create formations in the sky.

The Golden Knights open their parachutes when they are between 2,000 and 4,000 feet (600 and 1,200 meters) above the ground. They then may perform more maneuvers as they float to the ground.

The Golden Knights' Mission

The Golden Knights perform for a reason. The U.S. Army needs new recruits every year. The Golden Knights perform at air shows to increase people's interest in joining the Army. They also demonstrate their skills by competing in national and international parachuting competitions.

Golden Knights perform other duties as well. They test new parachuting equipment. They also test new parachuting methods. The Golden Knights help find safer and better ways for people to use parachutes.

Goodwill Ambassadors

The Golden Knights are called the Army's "Goodwill Ambassadors." They represent the

Army by demonstrating their skills in the United States and around the world. The Golden Knights have performed in all 50 states. They also have performed in 48 foreign countries. They perform for nearly 12 million people each year.

The Golden Knights are stationed at Fort Bragg, North Carolina. The USAPT is divided into six sections. The aviation section has six airplanes. This section also includes pilots and mechanics. The headquarters section manages the team's budget, maintenance, and publicity.

The remaining four sections include two demonstration teams and two competition teams. The 12-member demonstration teams perform at air shows. The 10-member competition teams participate in competitions.

The Golden Knight competition teams have won more competitions than any other U.S. military sports team. They also have won more competitions than any other parachuting team in the world.

Golden Knight Insignia

The parachute on the Golden Knight insignia is similar to the conquistador parachute. The Strategic Army Corps Sport Parachute Team helped design this parachute.

The knight's helm represents the USAPT's conquest of the skies. Golden Knights are able to safely jump from airplanes and free fall through the sky.

Chapter 2
Golden Knights' History

In the 1950s, Eastern European skydiving teams won most skydiving competitions. U.S. Brigadier General Joseph Stilwell wanted to change that fact. Stilwell was Chief of Staff for the XVIII Airborne Corps. This unit was stationed at Fort Bragg. Stilwell wanted to form a parachute team that could perform as well as Eastern European skydiving teams.

STRAC
Stilwell recruited 13 Army paratroopers for the team. These soldiers were trained to jump out

Paratroopers train to jump out of airplanes.

of airplanes to reach battle sites. They formed the Strategic Army Corps Sport Parachute Team (STRAC). Some of these paratroopers had been members of the 1959 All-Army National Team. This team had finished fourth at the Adriatic Cup skydiving competition in Yugoslavia.

STRAC's mission was to promote the Army's image and aid in recruiting. At the time, many people thought skydiving was more for entertainment than for sport. STRAC members visited cities throughout the United States. They showed people the skill and training needed for skydiving. STRAC members also competed in international competitions.

STRAC's first year of performing was 1960. That year, the team won three gold medals at the National Skydiving Championships. At the World Skydiving Championships, they placed fourth. One team member won an individual gold for his performance. He was the first U.S. parachutist to win a gold medal in an international competition. Another STRAC member scored the first dead-center

Parachutists try to hit a small target with their heels during accuracy competitions.

landing at a world championship accuracy contest. For this event, a parachutist tries to land on a target that is about 16 feet (5 meters) wide. The target's center is slightly more than 1 inch (3 centimeters) across. Competitors try to hit the target's center with their heels.

Between competitions, STRAC members toured the United States and three foreign countries. Their public appearances gained them respect and a loyal following of fans.

The Golden Knights

On June 1, 1961, the Army recognized the team as the official U.S. Army Parachute Team. The team then gained new members and new duties. The USAPT began to test and develop free-fall parachuting methods for military use.

By the end of 1962, the USAPT had earned the nickname "Golden Knights." "Golden" referred to the gold medals that the team had won in competitions. "Knights" was chosen as a symbol of their skill.

The Golden Knights' Popularity

In 1963, the USAPT expanded. More people wanted to see them perform. The 51-member team split into two demonstration teams and one competition team. The two demonstration teams were called the gold and the black teams.

The Golden Knights also received their own aircraft to use during performances. Pilots and mechanics then joined the team to operate and maintain these aircraft.

The Golden Knights' expansion helped their success. In 1964, they finished first in the World Skydiving Championship.

The USAPT had to expand because many people were interested in seeing them perform.

The first woman joined the team in 1977. Cheryl Stearns had already won a National Skydiving Championship when she enlisted in the Army. A year later, Stearns won the women's World Skydiving Championship.

The Golden Knights' popularity continues to grow. They have performed more than 8,500 times. They have performed at special events such as Major League Baseball games and National Football League games. They have even participated in a world-record 60-person formation.

Presidential Jump

During World War II (1939–1945), enemy fire damaged the airplane George Bush was flying. He and his crew bailed out. But Bush opened his parachute too soon. His head hit the airplane's tail wing. The wing tore part of his parachute. Bush was lucky to survive. After his accident, Bush decided that he wanted to parachute again someday and do it right.

In January 1989, four Golden Knights parachuted at Bush's presidential inauguration ceremony. They landed near the Lincoln Memorial in Washington, D.C.

Eight years later, Bush traveled to the Yuma Proving Ground in Arizona. The Golden Knights train there during the winter. The former president spent six hours training with team members. The next day was his 75th birthday. He parachuted with several Golden Knights. After an 8,000-foot (2,400-meter) free fall, Bush opened his parachute. He landed safely on the ground and fulfilled his dream.

Golden Knights parachuted at George Bush's presidential inauguration ceremony.

Chapter 3
Parachuting

People have been designing parachutes for centuries. In 1495, artist Leonardo DaVinci designed a pyramid-shaped parachute. But historians do not know if DaVinci tested his design.

French soldier Andre Garnerin designed the first parachute that could hold a person's weight. His parachute was round in shape. In October 1797, a hot air balloon lifted Garnerin nearly 2,000 feet (600 meters) into the air. He then cut himself loose from the balloon and drifted downward. As he descended, Garnerin swayed back and forth. This motion made him sick. He also landed hard on the ground.

Early parachutists used round parachutes.

Drag and Lift

Like all round parachutes, Garnerin's parachute had a problem with too much drag. Drag is the force of air against a moving object. It is one of two forces that slows a parachutist's descent. The other force is lift.

Airplanes use lift to rise into the air. Lift is created by the flow of air over and under airplanes' wings. Air flows faster over the wings than it does under them. Slow-moving air under the wings has higher pressure than fast-moving air over the wings. High-pressure air moves toward the low-pressure air and pushes upward on the wings.

Drag slows a parachutist's rate of fall. But it also slows forward speed. Forward speed helps parachutists control the direction of their descent. It also prevents the swaying that Garnerin experienced.

Parachute Improvements

Parachutes have been greatly improved over the years. Golden Knights now use ram air parachutes. These parachutes are made of a strong, lightweight fabric called nylon. They are rectangular in shape. When open,

Ram Air Parachutes

In the 1960s, kite designer Domina Jalbert developed a parafoil kite. This type of kite has openings in the front or underside. Air flows into these openings and inflates the kite into an airfoil shape. This shape is similar to an airplane wing.

Parafoil kites work like airplane wings. They create lift by allowing air to flow faster over them than it does underneath them.

Jalbert's design was used to develop ram air parachutes. By the 1970s, many people began to use ram air parachutes instead of round parachutes. Ram air parachutes are much easier to control than round parachutes.

they act like an airplane's wing. A ram air parachute uses lift instead of drag to slow a parachutist's descent.

Speed is important when Golden Knights perform. Forward speed increases lift. Lift allows parachutists to have better control of the direction that they are traveling in. The Golden Knights' parachutes have an average forward speed of 22 miles (35 kilometers) per hour.

Two Dacron lines attach to the back of ram air parachutes. Parachutists hold these cords during their descent. Dacron lines help parachutists control their direction. A tug on the left line turns them left. A tug on the right line turns them right. Parachutists pull on both lines at once when they are about to land. This action slows both their forward speed and descent.

Safety

All parachutists must use a single harness, dual parachute system. This system has two parachutes. A reserve parachute opens if the main parachute fails.

Golden Knights pack their main parachutes. But reserve parachutes must be packed by

Golden Knights pack their main parachutes.

certified parachute riggers. These technicians
are trained to pack reserve parachutes. They
also perform parachute repairs.

Reserve parachutes have an automatic
activation device (AAD). This device senses
a parachutist's altitude. It opens the reserve
parachute at 750 feet (230 meters). The AAD
protects parachutists who are unable to open
their parachutes themselves.

Golden Knights consider safety their
number one priority. Their safety motto is,

Golden Knights free fall at speeds greater than 100 miles (160 kilometers) per hour.

"No jump is so important that it cannot be canceled or postponed."

The Speed of Free Fall

Each 30-minute demonstration takes three hours of preparation. This time includes practice on the ground. Team members must be sure that they know each maneuver. During free fall, they must not make mistakes. Mistakes can lead to serious injuries.

Golden Knights reach speeds greater than 100 miles (160 kilometers) per hour within 10 seconds after jumping. By moving their bodies, they can slow or increase how fast they fall. They lie flat to slow their descent. They stand upright or dive to increase their speed. With practice, Golden Knights can reach speeds of more than 200 miles (320 kilometers) per hour. During a performance, the average free-fall speed is 120 miles (193 kilometers) per hour.

Demonstration Team Maneuvers

The 12-member demonstration teams perform two types of shows. They perform mass exit and full show demonstrations.

The entire team jumps at the same time for a mass exit show. During their free fall, they join to form a circle. They then pull away from each other to open their parachutes. The red smoke from their smoke canisters forms a bomb-burst pattern.

During a full show, one or more team members jump at a time. The Golden Knights perform several types of maneuvers during these shows. The Cutaway is designed to show

Canopy relative work involves two or more Golden Knight team members.

what parachutists do if their main parachute fails. A team member wears two main parachutes during this maneuver. The parachutist opens the first parachute. This team member then makes the parachute fail by releasing the risers on one side of the parachute. These cords connect the parachute to the parachute container. The container is strapped to the parachutist's back. After the risers are released, the parachute collapses. The parachutist then unhooks

the failed parachute and opens the second
main parachute.

Two or more Golden Knights perform canopy
relative work (CRW). Team members perform
these maneuvers after opening their parachutes.
Canopy crew formations are one type of CRW
maneuver. After opening their parachutes, team
members join together. They may stand on top of
one another or side by side for these maneuvers.

Style and Accuracy Team

The Golden Knight competition teams compete
in different areas. Members of one team compete
in style and accuracy competitions.

Style competitions involve one parachutist.
This parachutist must perform six maneuvers
during free fall. These moves include two right
turns, two left turns, and two loops. Judges base
competitors' scores on the time it takes them to
complete the maneuvers. The maneuvers must be
completed within 30 seconds. Some of the best
parachutists can complete these moves within
10 seconds. Competitors also are scored on how
well they perform the maneuvers.

The Golden Knight free-fall formation team creates formations in the sky.

For accuracy competitions, parachutists jump at 2,500 feet (760 meters). They try to land on a soft landing pad. In the center of this landing pad is a target that is about 6 inches (16 centimeters) wide. Competitors are scored on how close they land to the target's center.

The Golden Knight style and accuracy team also competes in team accuracy competitions. During these events, four parachutists jump at the same time. They then try to hit the target's center one at a time.

Free-Fall Formation Team

The Golden Knight free-fall formation team competes in several categories. These contests include four-way, eight-way, 10-way and 16-way competitions. But the Golden Knights specialize in eight-way competitions.

The competitors perform a planned series of maneuvers during four-way and eight-way competitions. They attempt to do this within a certain amount of time. Four-member teams have 35 seconds. Eight-member teams have 50 seconds. If they have extra time, teams repeat the maneuvers. Teams are judged on how many maneuvers they complete during the given time.

Ten-way and 16-way competitions involve 10 and 16 parachutists. These parachutists try to form a pattern as they free fall. Each team is judged on how quickly it forms the pattern.

The Golden Knight free-fall formation team has been very successful. During the 1980s and 1990s, they won the four-way world championship seven times. They won the eight-way world championship six times in a row.

Chapter 4

The USAPT

Fort Bragg is located near Fayetteville, North Carolina. This large Army post is home to the XVIII Airborne Corps and the 82nd Airborne Division. The USAPT is the post's smallest unit. It also is the U.S. Army's only demonstration team. Six remodeled World War II barracks serve as the team's headquarters at Fort Bragg.

All USAPT members began their Army careers as soldiers. They may have trained to drive tanks or control air traffic. Others may have worked as military police or infantry. These soldiers train to fight on the ground. But

The Golden Knights are the U.S. Army's only demonstration team.

Golden Knights often jump out of C-31A Troopships during demonstrations.

each Golden Knight team member performs an important duty.

Headquarters and Aviation Sections

The Golden Knights' headquarters section performs support duties. Operations staff members schedule air shows. Supply staff members make sure that the team has the equipment that it needs. Recruiters travel with the demonstration teams. They talk to people interested in joining the Army. Media relations

staff present information about the Golden
Knights to the public. Riggers pack the
team's reserve parachutes and repair damaged
parachutes.

The aviation section transports the Golden
Knight parachutists. Golden Knight pilots use
several types of airplanes. These aircraft
include DHC-6 Twin Otters, UV-20A Pilatus
Porters, and C-31A Troopships.

Support personnel go through an in-depth
selection process before they can join the
Golden Knights. They are tested on their skills
and knowledge of the Golden Knights. Many
support personnel are former Golden Knight
competition or demonstration team members.
These people already know a great deal about
how the team works.

Competition and Demonstration Teams

Each year, about 45 Army members apply to
join the Golden Knight competition and
demonstration teams. The application asks
candidates about their military and parachuting
experience. Candidates must write a paragraph
explaining why they want to join the Golden

Knights. They also must have performed at least 150 free-fall jumps.

About half of the candidates are chosen to attend a six-week selection program. The candidates learn about the USAPT. They also learn how to perform all of the Golden Knights' maneuvers. Candidates are then tested on what they have learned.

Only about eight of the applicants become members of the Golden Knights. But this number depends on how many openings the team has. Golden Knights enlist for three years on the team. But they may be allowed to serve longer. They can perform with the team for up to eight years.

Training

The Golden Knights live and train off post. Fort Bragg has several drop zones for paratroopers to train. But these areas are used by Army airborne troops and Special Operations Forces. The Golden Knights would not be allowed much time to practice at these drop zones. They practice at non-military airports instead.

Golden Knights pack their own parachutes.

The competition teams use the skydiving center in Raeford, North Carolina. They have trained at this small, private airport for 25 years. Several times a year, they also travel to different drop zones throughout the United States to practice.

The demonstration teams train at an airport in Laurinburg, North Carolina. Part of the Golden Knights' selection program also takes place there.

Golden Knights perform at air shows between March and November.

From mid-January to mid-March, the Golden Knights travel to Yuma, Arizona, for winter training. There, they perfect their skills for the upcoming show and competition season. USAPT members make at least six jumps each weekday. They continually practice maneuvers.

The training site is open to the public. About 250 visitors come out to watch each day.

At the end of March, the air show season begins. The Golden Knights perform at more than 100 air shows each year.

The Dangers

Skydiving can be dangerous. But the Golden Knights are well-trained parachutists. Their training and safety measures help them avoid injuries.

But not all accidents can be prevented. A recent accident occurred February 6, 1994. Sergeant José Aguillon and Sergeant Dana Bowman were practicing the Diamond Track. During this maneuver, two parachutists attempt to draw a diamond in the sky with red smoke. Both Aguillon and Bowman had performed this maneuver many times.

The two parachutists exited separate doors of the airplane. They traveled about 1 mile (1.6 kilometers) in opposite directions during their free fall. They then turned toward each other to complete the diamond.

Parachutists usually pass close to each other during this maneuver. But this time, Aguillon

Dana Bowman continues to parachute despite his injury.

and Bowman crashed into each other while traveling at nearly 150 miles (240 kilometers) per hour.

The impact killed Aguillon. The impact also opened Bowman's parachute. He landed in a parking lot and survived. But he lost both his legs because of the accident.

After his accident, Bowman remained an active member of the Army. He also continued to serve with the Golden Knights as a media relations staff member. He no longer could perform with his teammates. But he did jump with them only 188 days after his accident.

The Golden Knights are proud of their safety record. They have performed thousands of jumps with few serious accidents.

Chapter 5
The Future

Today, the USAPT is the world's most successful skydiving team. The competition teams have collected many national and international awards. They have claimed the eight-way world championship in formation skydiving six times in a row. They also have won the national style and accuracy championship for three years in a row.

Each year, the Golden Knights perform more than 26,500 jumps. Their consistent performance displays their skill and talent.

The Golden Knights have won more parachuting competitions than any other team in the world.

A Recruiting Tool

In 1999, the Army assigned the Golden Knights to Recruiting Command. Since then, the team has been an effective recruiting tool.

Many people have been interested in the Golden Knights' new tandem program. During tandem jumps, specially trained parachutists jump with a passenger. These two people are connected by a harness and use a parachute designed for tandem jumps. This program helps interest people in the Army.

The tandem program began in 1998. Army officials offer new recruits, members of the media, and celebrities the chance to participate in this program. David Hasselhoff from *Bay Watch* and country singer Sherrie Austin have participated in the tandem program.

Jumping into the Future

The USAPT's schedule has become more and more demanding. In 2000, they scheduled more than 300 demonstrations. In the future, they may need a third demonstration team.

Tandem jumps involve two parachutists.

Together, the competition and demonstration teams will continue to perform and compete. Their skills demonstrate the training that they receive in the Army.

Words to Know

ambassador (am-BASS-uh-dur)—a representative of a group or country

aviation (ay-vee-AY-shuhn)—the science of building and flying aircraft

drag (DRAG)—the force created when air hits a moving object; drag slows down the object.

enlist (en-LIST)—to join the military

free fall (FREE FAWL)—the part of a parachutist's jump before the parachute opens

infantry (IN-fuhn-tree)—a group of soldiers trained to fight on the ground

lift (LIFT)—the force that moves an object upward

parachute (PA-ruh-shoot)—a piece of strong, lightweight fabric used to drop people safely from aircraft

paratrooper (PA-ruh-troo-pur)—a soldier trained to use a parachute

tandem (TAN-duhm)—a parachute jump made with two parachutists connected by a harness

To Learn More

George, Charles, and Linda George. *Team Skydiving.* Sports Alive! New York: Capstone Books, 1999.

Green, Michael. *The United States Army.* Serving Your Country. Mankato, Minn.: Capstone High-Interest Books, 1998.

Hopkins, Ellen. *The Thunderbirds: The U.S. Air Force Aerial Demonstration Squadron.* Serving Your Country. Mankato, Minn.: Capstone High-Interest Books, 2001.

Van Steenwyk, Elizabeth. *Air Shows: From Barnstormers to Blue Angels.* A First Book. New York: Franklin Watts, 1998.

Useful Addresses

International Council of Air Shows
751 Miller Drive SE
Suite F-4
Leesburg, VA 20175

**Professional Air Show Performers and
    Producers Association (PAPPA)**
P.O. Box 8458
Norfolk, VA 23503-0458

United States Army Parachute Team
P.O. Box 70126
Fort Bragg, NC 28310-0126

U.S. Parachute Association
1440 Duke Street
Alexandria, VA 22314

Internet Sites

Golden Knights-United States Parachuting Team
http://www.usarec.army.mil/hq/GoldenKnights/index.htm

International Council of Air Shows
http://www.airshows.org

U.S. Army Recruiting
http://www.goarmy.com

U.S. Parachute Association
http://www.uspa.org

Index